Blackstone House Publications

TEACHING

The House of Ibn Kathir -
Yemen Plain

(Book 2 of the House of Ibn Kathir series)

S N Jalali

BLACKSTONE
HOUSE

First published in Great Britain in 2019 by Blackstone House
Publications, PO Box 1091, Harrow, HA1 9HG
www.blackstonehouse.com

Revised edition published in Great Britain in 2020
by Blackstone House Publications

Copyright © text Blackstone House Publications 2020
Copyright © cover illustrations and interior art S N Jalali 2020

The moral right of the author has been asserted.
All rights reserved. No part of this publication may be reproduced
or transmitted by any means, electronic, mechanical, photocopying
or otherwise, without the prior permission of the publisher.

With the exception of historical figures, all the characters in this
book are fictitious, and any resemblance to actual persons, living
or dead, is purely coincidental. All Islamic content has been
verified and every effort has been made to ensure that Qur'anic
translations and words attributed to the Prophet Muhammad
PBUH are from authenticated sources.

This book is sold subject to the condition that it shall not, by way
of trade or otherwise, be lent, re-sold, hired out or otherwise
circulated without the publisher's prior written consent in any
form of binding or cover other than that in which it is published
and without a similar condition including this condition being
imposed on the subsequent purchaser.

A CIP catalogue record of this book is available from the British Library

ISBN 978-0-9569000-5-0

Printed and bound by CPI Group (UK) Ltd, Croydon, CR0 4YY

Typeset in Baskerville

Other titles available

The House of Ibn Kathir – The Competition Begins

The House of Ibn Kathir – Year Captain

The House of Ibn Kathir – The Competition Begins Teaching Resource

All of the above titles are available to purchase from the website www.ibnkathir.co.uk

Also available from the website are free downloadable worksheets that accompany the teaching resource books, under the relevant teaching resource purchase page.

Please visit www.ibnkathir.co.uk for more information.

The Prophet Muhammad (peace be upon him) said, "Allah makes the way to Jannah easy for him who treads the path in search of knowledge."

[Muslim]

CONTENTS

Introduction to the House of Ibn Kathir	1
English Language	6
Poetry Analysis	9
Writing Technique - Mirroring	11
Writing Suggestions	12
Group Activities	14
Discussion Points	15
Religion	20
Field trip Activity	29
Leadership Skills	32
References	34

INTRODUCTION

The House Of Ibn Kathir - Year Captain

It's Yusif's second year at Dar Al Ilm Academy. Leaving home again, especially after the arrival of his new baby sister Aasiya, wasn't going to be any easier for him than it had been before. But after last year's adventures at his new school - which threw unexpected twists and turns his way, the unravelling of mysterious events with his new friends Reda, Warsoma and Daud beside him, and being called to stand as Year Captain - Yusif is eager to go back. However, not long after taking his first steps back into the Great Hall, Yusif's excitement at starting school begins to wane, as the responsibility of Year Captain grows heavy upon his shoulders. He soon wonders if he's really cut out for the job. First there is a disastrous orienteering trip, where his team comes last at the competition line under his poor leadership. Then, there are arguments and broken friendships that he faces over plans to raise money for Sheikh Ansari's 'mystery plans' for the school. Navigating his way through school as Year Captain proves to be a challenge that Yusif had never expected.

But all is not lost. With the help of his best friends and the return of a familiar old face from the past, Yusif rises to the challenge and begins to take charge, aiming to bring home the Captain's Cup. By organising a hair-raising event that saves the 'mystery plan', he gives the school a jaw dropping sports spectacle at the Lower Fields, the likes of which they have never seen before. The event is sure to leave the school talking about it for years to come as its best ever.

Use in Curriculum

This teaching resource has been produced to sit alongside any English curriculum and across Islamic studies, ethics or personal social development classes. The aim of this resource is to enrich the experience of reading The House of Ibn Kathir - Year Captain by suggesting starting points for students to reflect and initiate discussion, writing, research and activities. This teaching resource is also designed to help students navigate their way to understanding the text as well as to appreciate the Islamic concepts they encounter as they read along.

Included in this resource are individual, group and class activities, and a range of writing tasks for different purposes.

Themes explored:

- ✓ religion
- ✓ family
- ✓ education
- ✓ boarding school
- ✓ friendships
- ✓ forgiveness
- ✓ leadership
- ✓ excellence

English Language

In this section, you can explore some of the language styles used by the author.

Discuss the writing style of the author. Consider the following questions to help explore the issues:

1. Look at the chapter titles. Why do authors use chapter titles? What does the author need to consider when choosing a title?

2. Choose a scene. What are some of the writing skills the author uses to set the scene?

3. How does the author create tension?

4. What kind of language techniques does the author use to keep the reader wanting to read on?

5. In CHAPTER 4, *The Unbreakable Promises* (p.54) Yusif remembers his time in the tunnels the previous year. How does the author create a memorable image of the tunnels?

6. How well constructed is this novel? *(Do the sequence of events run naturally from one to the other? Are there any subplots?)*

7. Does the author create convincing characters and, if so, how?

8. Trace the development of the relationship between Yusif and Khalid. What significance does it hold, if any?

9. What are your impressions of Khalid in this book?

   (In some ways, compared to other characters Khalid is more realistic than some of the other characters. How does his character relate to the outside world? Why is his character important?)

10. What are some of the themes explored in the book?

11. Within the The House of Ibn Kathir – Year Captian, there are many stories about various Prophets through history. Why do you think the author weaves them into the plot? Do they have relevance for us today?

Discussion prompts during reading

Making predictions is a useful strategy in establishing the understanding of the student about the text that has come before. They can use information from the story so far, including subplots, characters, headings and pictures, as well as using their own personal experiences to anticipate what may be about to unfold in the novel.

What do you think will happen next?

1. At the end of CHAPTER 5, *Lost Boys* (p.56). The boys are scared of a disturbance in the nearby thicket. What do you think is going to happen?

2. At the end of CHAPTER 11, *Decisions, Decisions*, (p.155) Reda storms out of the emergency meeting. What do you think will happen next?

3. In CHAPTER 19, *Rewards All Round...* (p.288) when Reda learns that his rival Hamza Hameed has won, he walks up to him after he receives his trophy. What do you think Reda will do?

Poetry Analysis

Look at the poem overleaf, 'Al Wudu' from CHAPTER 16, *All in the Preparation* (p.249).

a. Explain briefly what you think the poem is about.

b. Identify the purpose, theme or message of the poem.

c. Does this theme appear anywhere else in the book?

d. Explore the emotions, moods or feelings expressed in the poem.

e. Identify the techniques used in the poem (such as form, structure, poetic devices and imagery).

f. What are your own thoughts and feelings about the poem?

g. Explore the differences between the features seen in poetry and prose.

h. Chose a favourite theme, character, scene or activity in the story and write your own poem.

Al Wudu
There's no finer key,
For it is the key to salah.
Al Wudu; sent to you and me,
That opens eight gates of Jannah,

If perfected, followed by prayer so sweet.
No nation before this was gifted like ours
The ritual that purifies faces, hands and feet,
Shining on the Great Day, brighter than stars.

The Beloved will gaze upon such radiance,
Knowing cherished followers from afar,
Ahead of those who showed obedience,
He waits at the spring of Al-Kawthar.

Thrice is the Sunnah of ablution,
Drops flow on face, arms, wipe head; and feet,
Pillars of purification, an expiation,
A blessing from our Creator, complete.

Ashhadu an la ilaha illallah, wahdahu la sharika lahu, wa ashhadu anna Muhammadan-abduhu wa rasuluhu.

Writing Technique – Mirroring

Mirroring is a technique in which an event, situation or a description is paralleled later in the novel by a very similar event or situation. There is some mirroring seen between the orienteering trip and the organisation of the *Triathlon of Sunnah Sports*. Compare and contrast Yusif's approach in the two different activities.

Writing Suggestions

1. In CHAPTER 17, *The Big Day* (p.265) Warsoma's brother Mahad can't come to watch the *Triathlon of Sunnah Sports* because he is climbing up Mount Kilimanjaro. Imagine you are Mahad and describe his experiences.

2. Write a news report about The House Of Ibn Kathir - Year Captain.

    ○ **Writing Objective A**
    Choose an event that takes place in the story and write a class news, news sheet or perhaps a news piece for Dar Al Ilm School bulletin.

    ○ **Writing Objective B**
    Summarise and report episodes from the book in a journalistic style, then swap with a partner and practise editing and proofreading skills.

    ○ **Writing Objective C**
    Discuss your favourite or more memorable parts of the book. Which might be particularly suitable for a newspaper-style report? You could consider:

- ✓ reporting on the orienteering trip – see CHAPTER 5, *Lost Boys* (p.56) and 6, *Sticks and Stones* (p.74)

- ✓ reporting on the highlights and results from the *Triathlon of Sunnah Sports* – see CHAPTER 18, *On Your Marks* (p.271)

- ✓ reporting on the success of the School Bazaar and the big announcement of securing the money needed for the completion of the Planetarium and Observatory – see CHAPTER 19, *Rewards All Round* (p.285)

Group Activities

Form small groups of 3 or 4. Each group should brainstorm and shortlist potential ideas for news items based upon earlier discussions (in Writing Suggestions task 2). Set a word limit (e.g. 200-250 words). Encourage groups to summarise in journalistic style exploring the features and techniques as seen in a newspaper. For example, short attention-grabbing headlines, appropriate styles of writing, informative for the reader, recounting events, interviews and use of short paragraphs. Look at different examples of real-life news pieces to get a feel for the style of writing required.

Presentation

Groups should decide how they will present their piece, e.g. it may be presented as a flyer, online news piece, printed newspaper, bulletin or school newsletter. How would they produce it, e.g. using a suitable software publisher or maybe hand-written?

Discussion Points

1. In CHAPTER 1, *Aasiya* (p.4) Yusif is at home with his family welcoming Ramadan. He has great plans for his month of fasting. What was the greatest challenge he faced? Why was it difficult for him and how well do you think he coped?

2. Consider the moon in Ramadan CHAPTER 1, Aasiya (p.8). What do you think Yusif saw in the night sky on his trips to the Mosque for *tarawih?*
   (This alludes to the changing phases of the moon through the course of the lunar month. Students can explore the lunar cycle and the relevance it has for Muslims with respect to the lunar calendar. How does the lunar calendar differ from the solar calendar? What are the Islamic months called? As an extension work, research significant events that took place during these months in Islamic history.)

3. Later in the chapter, Yusif is visited by Warsoma and Khalid at his home. Yusif and Khalid got off on the wrong foot in the previous year at Dar Al Ilm Academy. Yusif decides to give Khalid a second chance. Why do you think he did that? Was he right to do so?

4. In CHAPTER 1, *Aasiya* (p.4) Yusif's father tells the story of Aasiyah bint Muzzahim, the wife of Pharaoh, and Musa (as), whom she raised like her own son, after she found him on the River Nile.

    ○ From the text, discuss why she was made to be an example for humankind.

    ○ What kind of leader do you think Pharaoh was?

5. In CHAPTER 1, *Aasiya* (p.10) both Yusif and Warsoma have become firm friends with Khalid.

    ○ How do you think Khalid felt in the Great Hall, CHAPTER 2, *Back to School* (p.27) when he met Reda and Daud after the holidays?

    ○ Imagine you are Reda. Give your view of Khalid.

6. In CHAPTER 6, *Stick and Stones* (p.74) the boys' orienteering trip was a disaster from their point of view.

    ○ What do you think went wrong?

    ○ What could have been done differently that may have led to a more successful outcome?

7. One of the running themes behind the story is leadership.

- From the book, draw examples of good leadership and / or role models and explain why you have chosen these. Which qualities do you think made them so?

- In CHAPTER 9, *Council Convenes* (p.74) Yusif is relieved that Luqman has not been chosen as Head boy. Do you think Luqman is Head boy material? Explore the pros and cons.

- Yusif thinks that Luqman's ambitious drive held him in good stead when it came to securing his position on the Head boy team. Why do you think Luqman made the team?

- In CHAPTER 13, *Stable Master* (p.190) while talking to the Stable Master, Yusif 'shot Reda a look that said hey, exactly who's in charge here?' Why do you think he did that?

- How should those in charge be treated by those that follow them? Explain your reasoning why.

8. In CHAPTER 10, *The Legacy* (p.153) what do you think Sheikh Ansari means when he says to Khalid the following?

    - 'As a matter of fact, I very much like the choice of friends you keep these days.'

    - 'You, I and everyone have been given a wonderous ability to look inside ourselves, to change and strive to be a better person, to walk the better path if we choose to...'

9. What qualities do you think make a good friend and what qualities do you think make a bad friend?

10. In CHAPTER 19, *Rewards All Round* (p.288) why do you think Reda accepts his defeat and shakes hands with Hamza Hameed without any hard feelings?

11. Have you ever had a similar experience where you didn't succeed in something?

    o How did you feel and cope?

    o Is there anything you could you have done differently?

    o Looking back, how do you feel about it now?

12. In CHAPTER 9, *Council Convenes* (p.114) the boys celebrate *Eid Al-Adha* over a variety of celebratory meals from around the Muslim world. Historically when Islam spread to new lands, many local customs remained as long as they did not contradict the principles of Islam. For example, local cuisines remained unchanged provided that the ingredients were *halal* and did not contain the use of prohibited ingredients (such as alcohol or the meat of pig).

    o Name some of the dishes from the Muslim world mentioned in the book that were laid out in the Orangery for the boys in celebration of *Eid Al-Adha*. Can you match the regions they come from?

- Explore how *Eid Al-Adha* is celebrated in different regions around the world.

- How do you celebrate *Eid Al-Adha* with your family?

- What do you eat on *Eid Al-Adha*?

13. What are your impressions of Yusif, Khalid, Warsoma and Reda by the end of the story?

14. How important are values for the boys in guiding their decisions and activities?

    - Can you identify some important values that are mentioned or alluded to in the book?

    - What actions did these values lead to?

    - Discuss what values are important to you, and why.

Religion

In this section, we will consider some Arabic religious words, phrases and practices.

In the book Yusif and his friends often use words and phrases in their language and participate in common Islamic practices performed by Muslims. Using the glossary of terms at the back of the book (p.312-316), or through the help of the storylines as they appear, or even through your own independent research where applicable, fill out the following table stating their meaning and when you would use it. This can be done individually or shared as group work activity.

Arabic word /phrase/ practice	Meaning in English	Description	Example of when it is used in the book or in what context
Al-Kawthar			
Allah Ta'ala			

Arabic word /phrase/ practice	Meaning in English	Description	Example of when it is used in the book or in what context
Al-Musawir			
As-salatu khayran min a nawm			
Awrah			
Ayat al-Kursi		It is the 255th verse of *surah al-Baqarah*. It is often recited by Muslims to seek the protection of Allah (all praise be to Him).	
Barakah			

Arabic word /phrase/ practice	Meaning in English	Description	Example of when it is used in the book or in what context
Deen			
Eid al-Adha			
Eid al-fitr			
Hadeeth			
Iftar			
Ihsan			
Ikhlas			
Insha'Allah			

Arabic word /phrase/ practice	Meaning in English	Description	Example of when it is used in the book or in what context
Jannah			
Jazak Allahu Khair			
Kaaba			
Khushu			
Maqaam Ibrahim			
Masha Allah			
Mawrid			

Arabic word /phrase/ practice	Meaning in English	Description	Example of when it is used in the book or in what context
Miswak	A tooth cleaning twig from the branches of the Salvadora persica tree. It was the practice of the Prophet (saw) to use the tooth cleaning twig.	The miswak is a sunnah practice from previous generations. The Prophet (peace and blessings be upon him) said, "This is my miswak and the miswak of all the Prophets before me"	
Na'authu billah			
Qadr			

Arabic word /phrase/ practice	Meaning in English	Description	Example of when it is used in the book or in what context
Ramadan			
Sadaqa Jaariyah			
Suhoor			p.2 Yusif; 'Waking up in the early hours of the morning he partook of a suhoor of delicious food.'
Sujood			
Sunnah			

Arabic word /phrase/ practice	Meaning in English	Description	Example of when it is used in the book or in what context
Taqwa			
Tarawih			
Taqabbal Allah			
Umrah			
Zamzam			

Famous Women of Islam

A great deal of research was required prior to writing The House of Ibn Kathir – Year Captain, as the story refers to many famous historical figures or events from Islamic heritage. Now it's your turn to do some research …

In CHAPTER 1, *Aasiya* (p.11-15) we learn about four great women of Islam mentioned in a famous hadith narrated by Anas (ra): That the Prophet (saw) said; 'Sufficient for you among the women of humankind are Maryam bint Imran, Khadijah bint Khuwailid, Fatimah bint Muhammad and Aasiya the wife of Fir'awn.' **(Tirmidhi).**

- Research these famous women mentioned in the hadith (or just focus on one) and produce a biography about them based on what you have learned through a PowerPoint or poster presentation.

The Inimitable Qur'an

In CHAPTER 8, *A Gift for the Children* (p.111-113) and through Yusif's homework (p.306-311), the inimitable Qur'an and its miraculous nature is discussed.

Yusif learns about one of the miracles of the Qur'an; that its language style and form are unique and cannot be imitated.

Discussion points

- This style of the Qur'anic language *cannot* be replicated, being impossible to tell if it is poetry or prose, as it combines all elements, each to a level that surpasses any other writing. This concept can also be discussed and appreciated as an extension work to the earlier section of this teaching resource book under the chapter

Poetry Analysis. Here the poem *Al Wudu* is studied, and questions are asked. Explore the differences between the features seen in poetry and prose.

- When the Qur'an was revealed the mastery of Arabic language was at its peak.

- It was enough for some Arabs to hear the recitation of the Qur'an for them to embrace Islam, like Umar Ibn al-Khattab (ra). Those who didn't, at the very least acknowledged that the language of Qur'an was no ordinary phenomenon.

- The challenge in Qur'an 2:23 still stands. No human has produced language of its like.

Field trip Activity

Aids to understanding CHAPTER 6, *Sticks and Stones* (*p.74*)

Throughout history, travellers have used the sun, the moon and the stars as a means of ascertaining their direction of travel. The sun is very useful for this purpose, as it rises from the east and sets in the west, which makes it easy to find out which direction you are travelling (see illustration). Another useful fact about the sun, is that (providing you are in the Northern Hemisphere), then when it is at its highest point in the sky, its direction is south. Note: if you are in the Southern Hemisphere, the direction will be north.

Sun's movement (Northern Hemisphere)

However, if you want to find out where north is precisely without a compass, you will need a sunny day, a long straight stick, a clear flat ground, and a couple of stones to use as markers (see illustration).

1. Drive the stick in to the ground so it stands vertically, which should allow the shadow of the stick to become apparent. Place a stone on the ground at the far end of the shadow.

EASTERN DIRECTION
(SUNRISE)
LOOKING SOUTH
(MIDDAY)
WESTERN DIRECTION
(SUNSET)

1.
2.
3.
E
W
4.
S
N

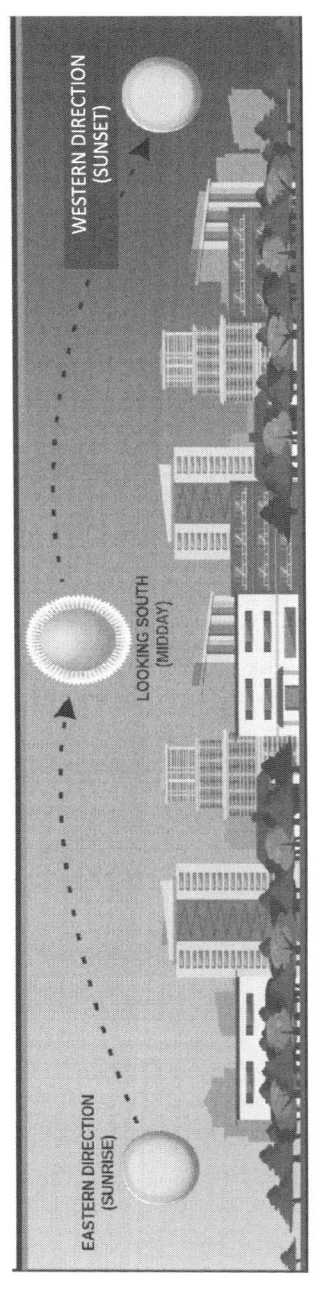

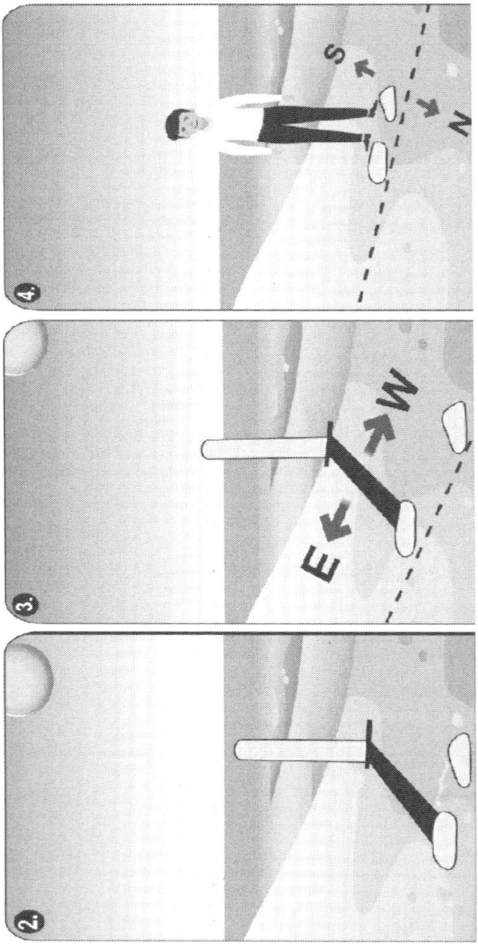

2. After 30 minutes has passed, the shadow would have moved away from the stone. Place a second stone on the tip of the new position of the shadow.

3. Using another stick, draw a line between the two stones. This line is an east-west line – the first stone is in the western direction, while the second is in the eastern.

4. If you stand with the line in front of you, with the first stone to your left-hand side, then you will be facing north.

5. If you want to find the direction of *qiblah*, turn 180 degrees anti-clockwise, you will be facing south; with an additional 45-degree turn, you will be facing south east (which is the direction of *qiblah* from England).

Leadership Skills

When people work in groups, there are a number of factors to consider when trying to make the group a success. To be a good leader it is important to consider some of the following aspects:

- ✓ Knowing the strengths and weaknesses of the group members

- ✓ Listening to and understanding the opinions of members of the team

- ✓ Respecting team members

- ✓ Being open minded and trying to find a consensus

- ✓ Making decisions in a decisive manner

- ✓ Keeping the team together, even if some members disagree

- ✓ Giving everyone a chance to participate according to their skills

- ✓ Be aware of the needs of each team member

- ✓ To be aware of one's own strengths and weaknesses

- ✓ Communications – giving clear and accurate instructions to team members

Discuss and contrast the above points in relation to Yusif and his friends' orienteering activities, and also in relation to the planning of the *Triathlon of Sunnah Sports* event.

References
(Note: Includes some further discussion points)

Qur'anic Ayats

CHAPTER 1, *Aasiya* (page 12)

> *'And Allah has set forth as an example, for those who believe the wife of Pharaoh: Behold she said: Oh, My Lord! Build for me, in nearness to Thee, a mansion in the Garden and save me from Pharaoh and his doings, and save me from those that do wrong.'* [Qur'an 66:11].

CHAPTER 4, *Unbreakable Promises* (page 54)

> *'So remember Me; I will remember you.'* [Qur'an 2:152]

> *'…If you are grateful, I will surely increase you [in favour] …'* [Qur'an 14:7]

> *'And your Lord says, "Call upon Me; I will respond to you."'* [Qur'an 40:60]

> *'…and Allah would not punish them while they seek forgiveness.'* [Qur'an 8:33]

CHAPTER 8, *A Gift For The Children* (page 113)

> *'And if you all are in doubt about what I have revealed to My servant, bring a single chapter like it, and call your witnesses besides God if you are truthful.'* [Qur'an 2:23]

CHAPTER 10, *The Legacy* (page 151)

> *'And it may be that you dislike a thing which is good for you and that you like a thing which is bad for you. Allah knows but you do not know.'* [Qur'an 2:216]

CHAPTER 12, *Old Boy* (page 186)

> *'(O Muhammad), whenever We raised any Messengers before you, they were no other than human beings; (except that) to them We sent revelation. So ask those who possess knowledge if you do not know.'* [Qur'an 16:43]

Note: Asking those of knowledge. In this chapter of the book (page 179) the previous Head Boy, Abdul Kadir returns to visit the school and finds Yusif in a dilemma over the *Triathlon of Sunnah Sports*. Yusif is confused as he has to make up his mind about the right course of action, while some of his friends are in disagreement, and he does not know enough to decide what the right answer should be.

Abdul Kadir quotes the above *ayat* of the Qur'an, which suggests that if one does not know, then one should ask those who do possess knowledge. While the Qur'anic ayat relates primarily to knowledge of religious matters, Abdul Kadir draws from this an analogy with knowledge in general terms. He suggests to Yusif that if he does not know something, he should consider asking someone else who has more knowledge in the field. For example, if someone was ill and wanted a cure for the illness, they would go to a doctor, who is learned in medicine, to seek the appropriate advice, rather than trying to treat themselves – which could have disastrous consequences!

CHAPTER 17, *The Big Day* (page 258)
Dua of Musa (as)

> *'Oh, My Lord! Let my heart be open to what is right and make my task easy for me and loosen the knot from my tongue, that they understand my speech.'* [Qur'an 20:25-28]

Note: (as) – Alayhi Salaam – May peace be upon him

Hadith References

CHAPTER 1, *Aasiya* (page 5)
Arguing whilst Fasting

Abu Huraira (ra) reported:
Allah's Messenger (saw) said: 'When any one of you gets up in the morning in the state of fasting, he should neither use obscene language nor do any act of ignorance. And if anyone slanders him or quarrels with him, he should say: "I am fasting, I am fasting."' **(Muslim)**

Discussion points from the novel:

- Why do you think Yusif found it difficult not to get angry when fasting?

- What are the lessons that can be learnt from fasting?

CHAPTER 1, *Aasiya* (page 8)
Gates of paradise are open

Narrated Abu Huraira (ra):
Allah's Messenger (saw) said, 'When the month of Ramadan comes, the gates of Paradise are opened and the

gates of the (Hell) Fire are closed, and the devils are chained.' **(Bukhari)**

CHAPTER 1, *Aasiya* (page 14)
The best of women

Narrated Anas (ra):
That the Prophet (saw) said: *'Sufficient for you among the women of mankind are Maryam bint Imran, Khadijah bint Khuwailid, Fatimah bint Muhammad and Asiyah the wife of Fir'awn.'* **(Tirmidhi)**

Discussion points for the story:

- What qualities did they possess that made them great women and therefore a role model for humanity?

- What were the stories of each of these great women? Choose one of them and write a short biography or make a presentation about their life either through a poster or maybe using PowerPoint slides.

CHAPTER 2, *Back To School* (page 29)
Prayer is better than sleep

It was narrated that Abu Mahdhurah (ra) said:
'I used to call the Adhan for the Messenger of Allah (saw) and in the first Adhan of fajr I used to say: 'Hayya 'ala al-falah, as-salatu khairun minan-nawm, as-salatu khairun minan-nawm, Allahu Akbar Allahu Akbar, la ilaha illallah

(Come to prosperity, prayer is better than sleep, prayer is better than sleep, Allah is the Greatest, Allah is the Greatest, there is none worthy of worship except Allah).' **(Nasa'i)**

CHAPTER 3, *Ismail Nasidi* (page 40)
Ihsan

On the authority of Abu Ya'la Shaddad bin Aws (ra), that the Messenger of Allah (peace and blessings of Allah be upon him) said about slaughtering an animal for food:

'Verily Allah has prescribed ihsan (proficiency, perfection) in all things. So, if you kill, then kill well; and if you slaughter, then slaughter well. Let each one of you sharpen his blade and let him spare suffering to the animal he slaughters.' **(Muslim)**

CHAPTER 3, *Ismail Nasidi* (page 40)
This is part of the long, famous hadith of Jibril AS

Umar bin Al-Khattab (ra) said: *'Once we were sitting in the company of the Messenger of Allah (saw) when there appeared a man dressed in very white clothes and having extraordinary black hair. No signs of fatigue of journey appeared on him and he was known to none of us. He sat down facing the Prophet (saw) leaning his knees against the knees of the Prophet (saw) and placing both of his palms over his two thighs and said, "O Muhammad (saw)! Tell me about Islam"…*
He then enquired: "Tell me about Ihsan." He (saw) said, "It is to worship Allah as if you are seeing Him; and although you do not see Him, He sees you."' **(Bukhari)**

Discussion points from the story:

- In the story Warsoma won the Ihsan cup for excellence and endeavour. Why do you think he won, and do you think he was a worthy recipient?

- Who else could have been a contender for this cup and why?

CHAPTER 3, *Ismail Nasidi* (page 43)
Giving gifts increases love

Abu Huraira (ra) reported that the Prophet (saw) said, *'Give gifts and you will love one another.'* **(Adab al-Mufrad)**

CHAPTER 5, *Lost Boys* (page 59)
Appointing a leader

Abu Sa'id Al-Khudri (ra) and Abu Huraira (ra) reported:
The Messenger of Allah (saw) said, 'When three persons set out on a journey, they should appoint one of them as their leader.' **(Abu Dawud)**

CHAPTER 5, *Lost Boys* (page 80)
Time of prayer

Ibn Abbas (ra) narrated that:
The Prophet (saw) said: 'Jibril (peace be upon him) led me (in Salat) twice at the House. So he prayed Zuhr the

first time when the shadow was similar to (the length of) the strap of a sandal. Then he prayed Asr when everything was similar (to the length of) its shadow. Then he prayed Maghrib when the sun had set and the fasting person breaks fast. Then he prayed Isha when the twilight had vanished. Then he prayed Fajr when Fajr (dawn) began, and when eating is prohibited for the fasting person. The second time he prayed Zuhr when the shadow of everything was similar to (the length of) it, at the time of Asr the day before. Then he prayed Asr when the shadow of everything was about twice as long as it. Then he prayed Maghrib at the same time as he did the first time. Then he prayed Isha, the later one, when a third of the night had gone. Then he prayed Subh when the land glowed. Then Jibril turned towards me and said: "O Muhammad! These are the times of the Prophets before you, and the (best) time is what is between these two times." **(Tirmidhi)**

CHAPTER 5, *Lost Boys* (page 87)
Place to pray

The Prophet (saw) said: *'The (whole) earth has been made a mosque (or a place of prayer) and a means of purification for me, so wherever a man of my ummah may be when the time for prayer comes, let him pray.'* **(Muslim)**

CHAPTER 7, *On Reflection…* (page 95)
Being stung twice

Abu Huraira (ra) reported: *The Prophet (saw) said, 'The believer is not stung twice from the same hole.'* **(Bukhari)**

CHAPTER 10, *The Legacy* (page 134)
Relieving a believer's distress

> On the authority of Abu Huraira (ra) from the Prophet (saw) who said, *'Whoever relieves a believer's distress of the distressful aspects of this world, Allah will rescue him from a difficulty of the difficulties of the Hereafter. Whoever alleviates [the situation of] one in dire straits who cannot repay his debt, Allah will alleviate his lot in both this world and in the Hereafter. Whoever conceals [the faults of] a Muslim, Allah will conceal [his faults] in this life and the Hereafter. Allah is helping the servant as long as the servant is helping his brother. Whoever follows a path in order to seek knowledge thereby, Allah will make easy for him, due to it, a path to Paradise…'* **(Muslim and Tirmidhi)**

Discussion points around the story:

- Helping others - the boys of the school work together to raise money – how successful were their efforts?

- Khalid's mistakes are hidden from the rest of the school. Why would that be important?

- The importance of learning.

CHAPTER 10, *The Legacy* (page 153)
Good and bad company

> On the authority of Abu Musa al-Ash'ari (ra), the Prophet (saw) said: *'A good friend and a bad friend are*

like a perfume seller and a blacksmith: The perfume seller might give you some perfume as a gift, or you might buy some from him, or at least you might smell its fragrance. As for the blacksmith, he might singe your clothes, or at the very least you will breathe in the fumes of the furnace.'
(Bukhari)

Discussion points around the story:

- Discuss the various friendship groups and rivalry between some of the boys.

- What personalities do some of the characters have that could make them a good friend to have?

CHAPTER 10, *The Legacy* (page 153)
Making mistakes

It was narrated from Anas (ra) that the Messenger of Allah (saw) said: *'Every son of Adam commits sin, and the best of those who commit sin are those who repent.'*
(Ibn Majah)

CHAPTER 11, *Decisions, Decisions* (page 166)
Cleanliness is half of faith

Abu Malik al-Ash'ari (ra) reported: *The Messenger of Allah (saw) said: 'Cleanliness is half of faith and Alhamdulillah (Praise be to Allah) fills the scale…'*
(Muslim)

CHAPTER 11, *Decisions, Decisions* (page 170)
Horse Riding, Archery and Swimming

> The Prophet (saw) said: *'Any action without the remembrance of Allah is either a diversion or heedlessness excepting four acts: walking from target to target (during archery practice), training a horse, playing with one's family, and learning to swim.'* **(al-Tabarani)**

CHAPTER 12, *Old Boy* (page 170)
Make wudu when angry

> Narrated Atiyyah as-Sa'di (ra): *AbuWa'il al-Qass said: We entered upon Urwah ibn Muhammad ibn as-Sa'di. A man spoke to him and made him angry. So he stood and performed ablution; he then returned and performed ablution, and said: My father told me on the authority of my grandfather Atiyyah who reported the Messenger of Allah (saw) as saying: 'Anger comes from the devil, the devil was created of fire, and fire is extinguished only with water; so when one of you becomes angry, he should perform ablution.'* **(Abu Dawud)**

Lie down when angry

> Abu Dharr (ra) reported: *The Messenger of Allah (saw) said to us, 'If one of you is angry when he is standing, let him sit down so that the anger will leave him. Otherwise, let him lie down.'* **(Abu Dawud)**

CHAPTER 13, *The Stable Master* (page 194)
Respecting elders

> Ibn Abbas (ra) narrated that the Messenger of Allah said:
> *'He is not one of us who does not have mercy upon our young, respect our elders, and command good and forbid evil.'* **(Tirmidhi)**

CHAPTER 14, *Hamra* (page 208)
The walking of the Prophet (saw)

> Abu Huraira (ra) said: *'I did not see anyone more handsome as Rasoolullah sallallahu alayhi wasallam. It was as if the brightness of the sun had shone from his auspicious face. I did not see anyone walk faster than him, as if the earth folded for him. A few moments ago he would be here, and then there. We found it difficult to keep pace when we walked with him, and he walked at his normal pace.'* **(Shama'il Muḥammadiyya)**

CHAPTER 14, *Hamra* (page 211)
Bad dreams

> It was narrated from Jabir (ra) that the Messenger of Allah (saw) said: *'If anyone of you has a bad dream, he should not tell people about how Satan played with him in his dream.'* **(Ibn Majah)**

CHAPTER 14, *Hamra* (page 214)
Giving something up for the sake of Allah

> It is reported from the Hadith of Abu Qatadah (ra) and Abud Dahma (ra) who said: *'We came to a man from the people of the desert and asked him, did you hear a hadith from the Messenger of Allah (saw)?' He said: I heard him saying, 'You will never leave something for the sake of Allah, but Allah will give you something better in return."* **(Musnad Ahmad)**

CHAPTER 15, *The Trials* (page 222)
Love for your brother what you love for yourself

> It was narrated from Anas bin Malik (ra) that: *The Prophet (saw) said: 'None of you has believed until he loves for his brother what he loves for himself.'* **(Nasa'i)**

CHAPTER 16, *All in the Preparation* (page 240)
Archery

> The Prophet (saw) passed by some people of the tribe of Bani Aslam who were practising archery. The Prophet (saw) said: *'O Bani Ismail! Practice archery as your father Ismail was a great archer.'* **(Bukhari)**

CHAPTER 16, *All in the Preparation* (page 249)
Dua after wudu

> Narrated 'Umar (ra):

Allah's Messenger (saw) said: 'If one after performing ablution completely recites the following supplication: (Ash-hadu an la ilaha ill-Allahu wahdahu la sharika lahu, wa ash hadu anna Muhammadan 'abduhu wa Rasuluhu)'I testify that there is no one worthy of worship but Allah, He is Alone and has no partner and Muhammad (saw) is his slave and Messenger', all the eight gates of Paradise will be opened for him and he may enter through any gate he wishes'. **(Muslim)**

CHAPTER 16, *All in the Preparation* (page 249)
Radiant faces

Narrated Nu'am Al-Mujmir (ra):
Once I went up the roof of the mosque, along with Abu Huraira. He performed ablution and said, 'I heard the Prophet (saw) saying, 'On the Day of Resurrection, my followers will be called "Al-Ghurr-ul-Muhajjalun" from the trace of ablution and whoever can increase the area of his radiance should do so (i.e. by performing ablution regularly).' **(Bukhari)**

CHAPTER 16, *All in the Preparation* (page 249)
Al-Kawthar

It was narrated that Anas ibn Malik (ra) said:
'One day when he-the Prophet (saw) was still among us, he took a nap, then he raised his head, smiling. We said to him: "Why are you smiling, O Messenger of Allah?" He said: "Just now this Surah was revealed to me: 'In the Name of Allah, the Most Gracious, the Most Merciful. Verily, We have granted you (O Muhammad) Al-

Kawthar. Therefore turn in prayer to your Lord and sacrifice (to Him only). For he who hates you, he will be cut off.'" Then he said: "Do you know what Al-Kawthar is?" We said: "Allah and His Messenger know best." He said: "It is a river that my Lord has promised me in Paradise."' **(Nasa'i)**

Note:

swt – Abbreviation for Subhanahu Wa Ta'ala – Glory be to Him, the Exalted

saw – Abbreviation for Sallallahu Alayhi Wa Sallam – May peace and blessings be upon him.

ra – abbreviation for Radiallahu Anhu – May Allah be pleased with him.

Famous sayings

CHAPTER 19, *Rewards all Round* (page 289)
Making seventy excuses

Hamdun al-Qassar, one of the great early Muslims, said: *'If a friend among your friends errs, make seventy excuses for them. If your hearts are unable to do this, then know that the shortcoming is in your own selves.'* **(Imam Bayhaqi, Shu'ab al-Iman)**